THROUGH THE SWAMPS OF TIME –

A COLLECTION

Other Books by Don Davison
An Outline of a Philosophy of the Consciousness of Truth
The Concept of Personhood in the Evolutionary Process of Being
The Game of Life: A Player's Manual for Executives and Others
Sign Posts: A Collection of Essays, Vol. I
Sign Posts: A Collection of Essays, Vol. II
Sign Posts: A Collection of Essays, Vol. III

Poetry
Thoughts and Feelings Book I
Thoughts and Feelings Book II
Needles from the Ponderosas at Zirahuen
Seeds from the Ponderosas at Zirahuen
Pitch from the Ponderosas at Zirahuen
Humus from the Ponderosas at Zirahuen
Sawdust from the Ponderosas at Zirahuen
Sun's rays through the Ponderosas at Zirahuen
Shadows beneath the Ponderosas at Zirahuen
Cones from the Ponderosas at Zirahuen
Pollen sifting from the Ponderosas at Zirahuen
Reflections from Lucerne
Searching Swamps
Questions
Time's Echoes
Memories

Collections
Always Extolling
Murmurings
Iris and Other Things
Pieces of the Journey

THROUGH THE SWAMPS OF TIME –

A COLLECTION

Don Davison

Zirahuen
Phoenix, AZ
pathtotheself.com
DrDavison@pathtotheself.com

©2010 by Zirahuen
All rights reserved. Published 2009
Printed in the United States of America

ISBN978-0-9774039-8-1

No part of this book may be used or reproduced in any manner whatsoever without written permission, except in the case of brief quotations embodied in critical articles and review.

Cover photo and author photo by Patricia Davison

Special thanks to Louella Holter, and to Tina Rosio, from W.

Again –
To Patricia, for everything.

All of Don Davison's books have water on their covers. Water is one of the most essential attributes of the planet Earth; without it, life as we know it would not exist. It deserves our most considered attention.

Davison's collections of poetry all end with "Finding Pieces." Many of you have asked, where did the rules for the Game of Life come from? They come from many places and different times. Good hunting!

CONTENTS

Dreams	1
RVM Requiem	2
Luna	4
The Mailbox	5
Tragedy	6
Wilber's Wonder	7
A Right	8
Age & Wisdom	9
An Act of Will	10
Change	11
Choose	12
Communication	13
Epitaph	14
Grandparents	15
Information	16
Through Leaves	17
A Symphony of People	19
The Wind	20
An Interruption	21
Change?	22
Messages	23
A Realization	24
Art	25
Bad Rap	26
Cayoosh Creek	27
Early Morning Thoughts	28
Eclipse	29
Fact	30

Gifts of Death	31
God Bless Those Who Marry Warriors	32
Greater Numbers	33
Humankind	34
I Remember	37
January	38
Just a Touch	39
Just People	40
Memory	41
The Hand Upon My Shoulder	42
The Present and Its Answer	43
The Wave	44
To a Shadow's Presence	45
To Sense	46
Tracks of Time	47
Watching	49
What is Important?	50
Which Crest?	51
A Few Good Men	52
Broth	53
Fact II	54
Flashing Visions	55
Going and Coming	57
How Can We Find Out?	58
I Write …	59
Listen!	60
True Religion	61
Negotiations	62
Our Cities	63
Permanence	64
Species Lost	65
The Blame Game	66
The Great Horned Owl	67
The Vet	69

Touchings	70
What Is That?	71
What to Do?	72
What Will Win?	73
Whispering Women	74
Who Will Say …?	75
Ode to an Urn	76
Shafts of Golden Light	77
Soul's Up!	78
A Life	79
Where Am I? Where Is It?	80
A Reminder	81
Broken Branch	82
Gifts of Life	83
God's Soul	84
It's a Yes! Now!	85
Others	86
Lumberjacks in Early Spring	87
My Last Wonder	88
A Tundric	89

DREAMS

Harsh, gentle, soft,
pulling, pushing,
masters of the heart.
Staunch haunting secrets.
Where do they come from?
How are they nurtured?
Is sharing possible?

RVM REQUIEM

The crucible is hot and white,
its contents vaporized in light.
Our souls sense and seek the night,
we close and dream of winning the fight.
How and when can we have
those glorious moments of peace?
Will warm sunrays heal headaches
as flights increase?
Has laughter ceased to swell the cabin
as twilight stills the movement of the day?
How long must we labor
with bills and expenses we cannot pay?
I'm tired and yet fulfilled,
the objective is within sight.
There is but one last effort
and then one last flight.
Whose schedule was the exercise on?
I never really knew.
Only faith in The Source, and in people,
gave us hope and carried us through.
Will the prize when won give birth
to moments lost and left undone,
as meetings consumed the hours
and left so little time for fun?
What was it that we shared
in the crucible along the way?
It could only have been the being of the self
as it exists day by day.
I wonder if the anger of absence will wane
with time spent seeking squirrels in the sight,
or as games are played and tickling
extends late into the night?

When does resentment begin?
Is it when I always say,
"I'm sorry, but I have to go and cannot stay?"
Maybe when it coincides with deeds
and growth I didn't see
it will cement the strength
to become their tree.
What is it in my eyes or yours,
success, joy, or just a dream?
The bottom line was always lemonade, not Coors,
and brownies with ice cream.
Dreams expressed or hidden,
whose burden do they become?
Does it matter if communication has been lost
and feelings have grown numb?
Time for them, for me, for us,
was it stolen, banked, or lost?
No one will ever know just how much
the whole exercise really cost.
The crucible is cold and blue,
its contents set in everlasting hue.
Our souls move and rise to the night,
we close and know we have won the fight.
The chalice of our sacrifices is overflowing.
We've placed them on the altar
still wondering where we're going.
As we turn from this moment
heading again up life's steep hill,
know that we dedicate ourselves
to Your Holy and Abiding Will.
Amen, alleluia!
Alleluia, amen!

LUNA

The rising, burning orb shares sustenance,
a sanctuary for the soul.
Passing lunar months feed the quiescent romantic
with the ephemeral and discrete.
Wavering luminosity,
now present, now hidden,
sets stages for that deep well of imagination
pumping images into being.
Reflections of soul
lie buried
within the eons of our pilgrimage.
In this endless now,
quest and repose,
– those twins of the diurnal –
fame and fortune,
the ecstatic and orgasmic
lure us into being's embrace.
Hush!
Be silent and remember!
Sense the essence of new-mown hay.
Touch with closed eyes the beauty of the present.
Nurture the effervescence of belonging.
Hold!
Adventure is at hand!
A keen urge swells the chest.
We mount the charger.
Dragons roam the land.
To both we owe
precious soul blood
dripping from our lifelong hourglass
into the sands of eternity.

THE MAILBOX

A canted home sits atop an old cedar post,
a wired iron bar as its spine
and piled stone its feet.
There sits a fancily decorated,
intimate expression of creativity.
What gifts may come?

TRAGEDY

Not to become a victim
of our own limited historical perspectives,
will always be the species' challenge.
To think we may be wrong
is the ever present
obligation.
In the flux of an ever new
presenting moment,
when we're always
"arising from,"
the challenge of the now
is to be heroic;
to greet each new circumstance
while remembering
we all want to believe in a better tomorrow
and to execute our commitment of will
with grace.
The tragedy is not to.

WILBER'S WONDER*

St. Thomas said it best,
"It's all straw!"
If you have too much of this and that,
you have nothing.
God's physics favors the simple man.
There's no need
for repetitions ad nauseam.
Quadrants, circles, spirals, spandrels,
ellipses, and graphics,
even tetrahedrons are add-ons.
They are all in the jack-in-the-pulpit,
the lady's-slipper.
Several questions to you, Wilber:
"What have you done with that star dust
in your center, or left of?
Or that moonbeam that passed
through your upper left yesterday?
Aren't these always with us
as we wait in joyful hope,
laboring our way on Mount Carmel,
seeking the beatific
as we go?"

*The author Ken Wilber

A RIGHT

That apex of human achievement
– so hard to reach –
the only place that matters
for us all,
calls from ahead
and is heard from behind.
What golden bow,
drawn with a pure heart,
loosed an arrow towards the truth
that lit the path towards Heaven's gate
where now,
forever,
we wander and we wait?
We live seeking that light upon the hill,
riding the cresting waves
of a deep welling.
Raising us higher and higher,
lifting us towards
a "More Than,"
calling us from the infinite to the eternal.
The message is clear,
"I am the Logos.
I am the soul of life."

AGE & WISDOM

Let me hear the panting of the old dog,
the blowing of the seasoned horse,
the shuffling of the aged lady,
the shrieks of grandchildren.
In this I will know
my life was not in vain.
With this my heart will rest in peace.

AN ACT OF WILL

From the psycho, physical depths
of our own history
and that of the universe,
we must force ourselves
to be still,
to be free.
Always still enough,
always free enough
to embrace
the beauty of the present.

CHANGE

The young knight
used to come back from his exploits
and conquests
and take the lady into his arms,
chemistry and images coursing through his head,
heart, and loins.
Now ...
The old knight returns
from long days and nights of idealistic
conquests of the evils of history,
or from the depression thereof.
With his pen
he tries to sow new perspectives
that will give birth to love and freedom.
Now
when he comes home,
he sometimes is too tired to
take his lady into his arms.
Yet the chemistry and images
are still coursing through his head,
heart, and loins.
So, he does!

CHOOSE!

Dawn's soft halo
breaks the wall of night,
bursting its brilliance
beyond the mountains,
edging darkness
over the far horizon.
Warmth's fingers grasp the day.
History's deeds flash from forgotten
snippets of awe and wonder.
To greet my time
the early sounds sift in, saying,
"Choose!
Choose!
Choose!"
Leaping from my resting place,
I choose to grip the day and mow the hay.
I choose to dance with God.

COMMUNICATION

Communication flows in omnipresent
particles and waves.
Encapsulated sight and sound
bequeath perceptions of relationships
of being to being.
The hominid,
amidst the whirlwind,
stands on the threshold of the present.
Accosted and caressed,
always wondering
what others feel and understand.
We see. We speak. We touch.
We hear. We taste. We smell.
The sea washes us in forever swirling
vortices of emotions –
those unfathomable depths
of human machinations.
Finally,
some form of understanding
bursts upon our consciousness.
We feel connected to a part of this raging sea.
Then,
in feeling full and awestruck,
tantalized by a faint hope of reciprocity,
desiring some fathomable interchange,
– only intermittently rewarded –
we attempt to share.

EPITAPH

A poet who writes in English
becomes aware of a dying tongue
and is cowed beneath the weight of knowing
he may be writing to lighten the load
of seeking souls in ever fewer
numbers.

GRANDPARENTS

It's time for us to walk the trails in the moss.
Yet …
We will also be there to scream for our grandchildren
at their testing and trying events.
And we will shout ecstatically
during their triumphs.
We will hug them
with the enthusiasm of teammates.
We will be there for them
as they rise to and beyond the occasions.
We will celebrate their trials and accomplishments.
We will laugh and we will cry.
And in our prayers
we will murmur,
"Thank you."

INFORMATION

Why do we hustle from cave to cave
to huddle and listen
and then go out again to see and do?
Lookers and seers
– how many doers are left?
Are those that sing in electronic song
giving meaning to the message?
Do we know by what we hear
that indeed the words are true?
Information tells us what?
How much do we need?
What do we really know
about this thing called information?

THROUGH LEAVES:
A REFLECTION ON THE QUICKNESS OF THE SEASONS

One of the beauties of swirling snow in midwinter
is that it does not have leaves
with which to contend
in drifting its way
into a blanket on the ground.
Of course,
there are times when it swerves around
a branch or bounces off a twig,
but in the main
it heads directly to the forest floor.
That isn't to say in some locales
it doesn't settle in a cluster of needles or branches
and build a puffy nest,
but in the hardwood forest
it gradually sifts its way to its final destination
incrementally covering all the leaves.
Those leaves ...
they should rest,
dangling as they do in spring
dressed in their soft, shiny pale green.
Then,
as time passes they stiffen,
and in a darker hue
riffle in the winds of summer.
Then they bend and break
in brittle battle
as Fall claims them for its carpet.
The winds rend and reap
sending leaves to the cellar
to be processed once again.

With brown, wrinkled lifeless leaves
and chilly fall rains,
the tomb remains
until snowflakes gently cover them
and press them one to one.
Ironed out they simply lie there
to feed the fertile soil
to start again the journey from the hollows
to the skies.
Now waiting as they do,
from dusk to dawn of life,
how interesting is their movement
from darkness to the light.

A SYMPHONY OF PEOPLE

From the soup of smog
the strings of an orchestra break forth
to say at least enough are present
to give support to the soul.
But because of the congestion is the music soothing,
restful, and creative?
And does it give us pause to reflect on the sufficiency of society?
Very few – some – many – a lot – too many –
Where is the health of the species today?
Is it in the cities of the globe?
There must be some
and yet I think we have moved
from wandering tribes to condensed urban centers
in too short a time.
A person needs to live alone with others
to progress through them
and out into a shared, integrated environ.

THE WIND

The wind,
tossing, turning, twisting,
soft, stirring, smashing,
buffeting, bellowing, blasting,
calm, churning, crashing,
pausing, pushing, puffing,
chilling, carrying, causing,
is the breathing of the world.
To touch the wind
is to sense the soul of the universe.

AN INTERRUPTION

The pristine silence is punctured by,
"I owe!"
Is there not some fundamental significance here?
What is my responsibility to the now?
Is it not to pray,
that is, to live in perpetual prayer
giving "Alabanzas" to the Most Holy?
Is it that I am in this crucible,
this vortex that shapes an altered time
and therefore precludes my knowing
the Holy in the present?
Or,
as with most false perceptions,
I choose to deny His Presence
in an egocentric focus on my now?

* * *

"Not my will, but Thine, be done!"

* * *

Silence reigns supreme across the eternal face
of time as His Radiance,
casting a brilliant glow on the now,
is finally seen.

CHANGE?

Will there be some who will find
"The Mancha" of their origins?
There is not much that distills from
the history of human effort.
Most of the pulp of the day fades into humus.
But,
there are those pristine moments when
a soul shines throughout the ages.
Thank you, Cervantes!
The ideal still battles with the real.
Thank you, Heraclitus!
The winds blow – the water rises.

MESSAGES

Doubt reigns supreme!
The fire of pride fans fear's flame.
The fare we feed our children
is fodder for their souls.
Rococo is dissonant, an assault on senses.
Those who glorify tragedy
with inappropriate art forms,
inappropriate subjects,
inappropriate circumstances,
sing Satan's song.
We are lost as we cross over the bridge
of ***Mine! Theirs! Now!***
With vile obscenities assailing
the innocence of children,
we say we love them.
"You insidious bastards of ignorance,
you defile the word ***Child.***"
May we be wise enough to know:
Eternal vigilance, Oh Lord!
Abba,
Eternal Vigilance!
Eternal Vigilance,
Oh Love!

A REALIZATION

When I am alone in the sacred silence of myself,
it is then that I honor the sacred silence
that accompanies all things.

ART

The arts are those magnificent creations
flowing from
heart, hand, and mind
to be shared with others.
They become a communal meal,
shared dining,
providing another course,
adding more flavor to the human experience.
At times presaging understanding,
or remembering
the best of times
and the worst of times.

BAD RAP

Does an incessant, syncopated rap
have to be part of every soundtrack?
Does truth stop at a river?
Not hardly!
How can we know
when convenience,
or some supposed politically correct
personal perspective,
does not measure up to the truth?
I have never heard
from so many
such pontifications of ignorance.

CAYOOSH CREEK

Where does God live?
From the eons of recorded history
sifted efforts of our kind
offer scant solace.
Armed with determination and aplomb,
a righteous stance assumed,
faces of smiles and tears
birth awe and dreaded vistas.
Still,
lingering ruminations lead us
in silent moments
to ask again the questions of the ages.
I can't hope to sway the hearts and minds
of fellow souls,
yet beyond any doubt,
I know that in the turns amidst
the placid stretches and racing rapids
of Cayoosh Creek,
mountains in mirrors and white rushing water
reflect and create emanations
that display eternal truth:
He lives here!

EARLY MORNING THOUGHTS

For who waits the linened table
with candles set aflame before the wall,
a wall where hangs a silver bell
that marks the moments,
and a mirror reflects a silent gaze
as morning's early light
sheds its glow on sea shells
hung beneath a cherub's lanterned shoulders,
where hands hold the sacred water for us all,
and where sits the maiden's wondering presence
touching truths of life's portent?

ECLIPSE

As I sit huddled in my chair at Rancho Aguililla
awaiting the eclipse of the moon,
I think of the Aztecs and Mayas
as they stood, squatted, or sat,
witnessing the same event.
In the moon's fullness,
then subdued state,
I wonder if we will have that moment
of advantage on the battlefield,
or whether there are any other "primitives"
still left
who have semi-pure wonderments
of causes and effects
hidden in the sky's events?
Pine branches dance in the moon's face
unaware of any difference.
While not of a sudden,
a gradual coming of a giant shadow
stalks the moon,
I stare at an earthly turning
of the cosmic tables.
Coyotes yip and dogs bark
as the shadow catches its prey,
and I wait
the unveiling of a new moon.
In this time-given gift
of the eternal dance of all things,
I sense an immense beauty
and feed myself a dessert
of faith, hope, and charity.

FACT

Many more artists and artisans
create things of beauty,
than terrorists
fabricate bombs.

GIFTS OF DEATH

They are born alone into their womanhood.
It does not matter what slang you spew,
how you saunter,
or what cultural blinders you choose to wear.
When your women become
wise enough to know
and possess sufficient wherewithal,
those of you who care not enough to listen,
you slime, you lecherous pigs of humanity,
will be welcomed to sudden power shifts
that will surely foretell
of your coming cultural deaths.

GOD BLESS THOSE WHO MARRY WARRIORS

The heroics of those who marry warriors
is the stuff of goddesses and angels.
To love enough
to allow one to follow one's own sense of duty
is to recognize a purpose
that meets the demands of human life.
When one considers the disposition of a lover,
a father, a mother, a provider, a friend,
a child,
we are not easily satisfied.
Our internal wish and our eternal desire
is always to share a presence with our love.
Yet in the face of an eclectic fleeting now
we still forge bonds with sufficient freedom
to allow warriors
to risk it all to protect beliefs
and place their lives
upon the altars of our times.

GREATER NUMBERS

Greater numbers are real
and made even more real by the media.
Yet ...
the whole remains the same.
The new smog of our time
presents only more of a few,
and that focus bends the perception of truth.
Media dumps information
into the whole,
and many believe the fare.
Who is it that really knows
what was and is
eternally already there?
Only those who see
the unmediated beauty
of the present.

HUMANKIND

From the eons of the hinterlands
comes the movement of our kind.
Growth-in-time gives
to each the opportunity to be-come
who and what they really are
in the context of their time.
A family is a holy sanctuary,
the beginnings of ourselves.
From ties that bind us to who and what we are
– almost –
to flowing matter,
free to choose
to mix and love another.
Slowly
enough of everything presents itself
allowing for a giving of each other to ourselves.
Fast enough to respond to the winds of flux,
respecting primeval laws,
blending,
be-coming one with others.
Learning to love
THE ALL
as death provides new opportunities.
An annual ring,
then new growth
a strength of seasons
rededicates to purpose.
A family shrine
for Abba.
"Lech heim!"

Conjugal love,
labor's pain,
children appear as soft bundles of new life.
Both are fine.
Relief.
Demands.
Hours of fatigue,
ecstasy,
pride,
disappointments,
lessons,
deeds,
broken moments,
flares of anger,
repose of compassion,
future's dreams,
tomorrow's hopes.
Everything expressed in them,
through them, by them.
Sacred sounds of increasing humanity
following the wisdom of the Greeks:
"It is better to be than not to be."
We populate the land.
Passing the torch of life to others
slow enough to share the learnings of our kind.
Respectful of history's deep commitment
for us,
for them,
for theirs,
for the world.
The species becomes,
the movement of our kind.
We have washed the shores of circumstance
and mingled in incessant interchange,
all colors, shapes, and sizes.

Contours of cultures' variegations
whipped the winds of change.
Too fast?
Too many?
Too slow?
Not enough?
The hominid has always followed
organic movement
– usually slow and methodical
– be-coming aware of resource interface,
eventually moving appropriately.
And, finally,
embracing some of what spirituality
has to teach us,
we are just now beginning to learn to love.

I REMEMBER …

"Who are you?"
"I'm the one who shot chipmunks in the spring
with my slingshot."
"And why in God's name would you do that?"
"Well …
"Should I answer from my now or my then?"
"Nothing you say could justify doing that!"
"I wanted to be like the trappers of old
and trade my skins,
the skins of the chipmunks for marbles."
"How could you do that?"
"All the boys were playing marbles.
I wanted to play too.
I had no marbles.
I shot chipmunks in the spring."

JANUARY

Geese are in the lowlands,
ravens on the hill.
Old Glory flutters from her pole.
A weather front has passed to no avail.
January is perched below the Arctic trough.
Lagging efforts of the season's joys
have yet to feel the nudge of Spring.
Politicians grope for any perch.
The economy slumbers,
as any healthy thing should do.
Worries ebb and flow.

JUST A TOUCH

When my whole being touches
the truth of my existence
in a sentiment of eternal gratefulness
and unbounded awe,
I utter my most profound prayer:
"Oh Great Lover of Life,
You have given my me to me,
again!
and now,
again!
I know Your Presence
in all things.

JUST PEOPLE

When do we realize
we are all just people?
We are not ideologues.
(They are so few.)
People are so many –
and all we want to do
is to live day to day,
to enjoy
the simple gifts of life:
A forthright self,
a loving mate,
honorable children,
work to be done,
and understanding friends.

MEMORY

"T-80235"
Just a memory? No!
It is one of my earliest commitments
to responsibility
and to the instructing abilities of my father.
Leaving the Ranger Station
in a fire truck,
the rapture of a Spring drive,
lacy leaves, warmth,
his presence.
Then ...
"Get that license number!"
An urgent tone, purposeful and intent,
from a man of few words,
"Dave, The Ranger,"
my father had spoken.
I read the plate.
Repeating the letter and numbers over and over,
I memorized them.
And here, some 58 years later,
I still see the car and remember the number.
Impact and life form,
T-80235.
What makes a person who they are
and who they become?

THE HAND UPON MY SHOULDER

The trail is long
in moments of the remembered and forgotten.
What pushes or pulls us forward,
leads us into pools of perdition
or raging flames,
believing we know
what's best for self and others?
Is it snatches of dreams and nightmares?
We are driven and repulsed.
We love and we hate.
A barely conscious mist of memories,
is that the only push?
Or,
must a deeper drive connect us to ourselves?
We search and search for answers.
Seldom do they come
and then only in flashing vistas
of "the right."
We are more than because we care.
We are tied to ourselves and we love another.
It must be Charity
that drags us
from the depths of confusion and perdition,
setting us on a path of forever sharing.

THE PRESENT AND ITS ANSWER

Still they say,
"Fax it!
Text it!
It'll be recycled on that end.
They'll answer us back.
Stay quiet!
Sit under the tree.
Work is to be done.
How much do I need
to build a washing machine,
a phone,
home,
car,
bicycle,
a bed?"
And finally,
"Can one person do all this
and still have time to love self and the world?"
Growth into the heart of God,
the eternal mosaic,
will be our only epilogue.

THE WAVE

"Which one was it?"
"That third one,
the one that rolled in
at the 7th hour on March 3rd, 931 AD.
I remember its crest tumbling into the sand,
flashing a spectrum's remnants,
foaming and sparkling
in the early morning sun."
"But there have been so many ..."
"Not like that one."
"What made it so special?"
"I was there,
and I saw it for the first time."

TO A SHADOW'S PRESENCE

It was a time of punctilious hubris.
So common,
just past the leading edge,
the one that gives direction
to our purpose.
It was a cratered moment
when lost in self-centeredness,
I forgot "the others."
To Octavio, to Martin, both of them,
to Teilhard de Chardin, and to Ortega,
to a very long litany,
and to you,
especially you,
Patricia,
the one who walked with me,
to you I owe so much.
And my
"Thank yous"
– the ones I truly meant –
were always breathed when I became aware
of your shadow.

TO SENSE

There was a time when Angels sang
and Dragons feasted on the flesh of men.
Where rest now the wishes of the soul?
In the chaos of times
we forget the omnipresence of peace
flowing in cosmic events.
Yet in our breathing
we can catch serenity
passing in and passing out,
giving us
the shining gift of life.
With eyes to see, a nose to smell, ears to hear,
fingers to touch and a tongue to taste,
we wage battle with our minds.
Great syntheses swirl in light and shadow.
A nectar's essence sweeps the nose.
We fathom the presence of a rose.
What other wonders
seep to the surface of our senses
begging to be held, to be cherished?
We waste such precious moments
when in angst we sink in despair,
ignoring great places of silence
serving banquets to starving souls.

TRACKS OF TIME

Every country's history
comes with tracks through swamps of shame.
The trees of national cohesion
derive their heartwood
from blood let by committed ideologues
using others for their fodder.
Seldom are the cries of liberty
only from those who write the pamphlets.
The expendability of human life
– when there are so many
and so much to gain –
has been a common choice.
In our present moment the mandate:
Money now!
has caused a bloodletting that shames us all.
A seductive necessity
has bound itself to the woof and weave
of every culture.
Millions pass away
with hardly a blip on the film of conscience.
The myopic glance at any others
was always clouded by an existential naiveté.
To know enough to survive
in our own little corner of the world was enough,
wasn't it?
Or,
was it only when there were few of us
and we were separated by vast pieces of geography
did facts of the moment
demand a different approach
and with this,
a different level of integrity?

If one,
myself,
is at all endowed with reason,
I must apply the appraisal of my being
to all others,
least I lie to myself,
all others,
and my God.
In the shallow dishes of the sea's waves,
waves reflecting millions and millions
of human faces,
we bear witness to the destruction of the ages.
In a newfound awareness
we have finally come to know:
If we lose one now,
we must suffer an agonizing pain of indifference.
Behold!
Lest we forget those tracks of time.

WATCHING

Which cresting wave,
when rising from the deep,
lifts and dips its white cap
to the lee side
and falling back into the sea
winks
and knows it was me?

WHAT IS IMPORTANT?

When do we ever stand still
long enough to see how it is
that common minds view
what are considered by many
the mistakes of history,
mistakes that become glorious pedestals,
great cornerstones of time?
Maybe,
when we are overcome by a trembling
and an incomprehensible sweat.
Then we stand still long enough
to see a new beginning.
And yet …
if one does not feel like shouting
at the racing clouds
or rising moons
as they dance in the twilight,
what good are they?

WHICH CREST?

Where does the crest of a wave begin?
In the trough behind –
from the depths of the last wave.
The challenge is
to stand screaming into the cacophony of foam
in the leading edge,
or unite with others of like minds.
The choice is always
to be free.

A FEW GOOD MEN

I seek a few good men
who revel in the farthest reachings of soul.
And that is all.
I seek a few good men
whose senses bask in wholeness,
not a dreary, thin palette of an age.
And that is all.
I seek a few good men
astonished by their solitude who, touching femininity,
romance with reverence like kittens at play.
And that is all.
I seek a few good men
tested by war,
yet free to love all the children of the day.
And that is all.
I seek a few good men
enraptured with sufficient erudition
comprehending the eternity of the present.
And that is all.
I seek a few good men
possessing subtle humor offering
poignant relief of perceptions strung on the rack of irony.
And that is all.
I seek a few good men
who remember Martin.
No! The other Martin
of the conversations of *I and Thou*.
And that is all.
I seek a few good men
free of the click-clacking rhythm of the mind,
souls free in silent stillness sensing
Presence.
And that is all.

BROTH

To the broth of the day
we add delicious chunks of delight
and joy.
From this we draw our sustenance,
this becomes the soup of life,
the larder of our memories.
The silver gray of passing days
distills in memory's mist
chunks of yesterday,
and as we stumble upon them
senses peak
and a warmer heart,
our heart,
heats again that broth
giving us a taste of where we've been,
what we've done, yet hope to do.
Be bold!
Add more ingredients!
Try a different flavor now and then.

FACT II

From the depths of fatigue,
caught in a halo while screening facts
hidden in treasures of history,
I re-membered
lives are always an individual effort,
the ownership of one
as a part of a whole.
We live tied forever to local circumstance,
connected universally
to all of humanity's brothers and sisters.

FLASHING VISIONS

Flashing visions
hurl themselves against the screens of our minds.
Smashing into one another,
heat rises
leaving smoldering eyes
to bake in an incessant showering of sparks.
A vague awareness screams,
"These are the long-sought-after quarks
– they are real –
we now know them
up close and personal."
If we could only hold on to them
or at least see their tracks,
their trails in the white powder of the mind.
Suddenly
we feel our bodies jerk in some ungainly spasm
as we try to focus blurring visions.
Driven by the sparks
we twist and bend,
stomping and jumping in a misplaced race,
attempting to apprehend what was just there
and we hope
will be there again …
Thrown by winds whose screeching rush
slams us forever forward,
we wail in desperate hope.

Then,
bounding and bouncing
along a synaptic, electronic archipelago,
barely touching fuzzy land masses,
we wildly grope
in a semi-lit forever dawn, or dusk.
Lost in cataracts of time
from self and others,
we stare at relentless tracks of photons
searching for some semblance of stillness
in which to bathe
our battered and crushed souls.
Huddled in our Dolby-based echo chambers
shadows of sounds assault singed senses,
tracking back and forth,
rattling us in acute angles and vortices.
Panting and shaking,
we live struggling,
separated from St. John's Dark Night,
its light,
and its still point.

GOING AND COMING

We are the going and coming species,
always on our way.
And when we do sit still,
we rage at others –
going and coming.
Few of us
are able to sit silent
long enough to touch the
placid mirror of God's creation.

HOW CAN WE FIND OUT?

Dialog is education.
So …
what do we know?
What do we need to know?
How can we find out?
In the eclectically disconnected
postmodern world,
how much history do we need to know
to be sufficiently inspired
to deal heroically with the present?

I WRITE ...

I write ...
hoping the luck of the draw
will bring just the right words
(never close enough)
to describe my experience
and awaken from your lexicon
words that evoke,
and in so doing
form a bridge to your experience.
I write ...
to provide entertainment,
to give glimpses of wonder
that caught my attention,
fed my dreams,
and washed my soul with a cold shower
in which every droplet whispered,
"Yes!"
I write ...
because I want you to know
"Yes" moments make me cry and shout for joy.
From sudden touches to transforming rivulets
that coursing over a body
irrigate primeval roots
drawing them into a new time
and a different place
– again –
new shoots rising
from the depths of my soul.

LISTEN!

It has been said:
"You murdering bastards of your own serenity
will be crushed by monsters
and float on the wings of butterflies
in gentle winds.
The insignificance of your intransigence
will lie like powder on their wings."

* * *

And it has also been mentioned:
"You have spit in the face of
Allah,
The Compassionate,
The Merciful,
long enough!"

TRUE RELIGION

Monks and nuns
bow to their tasks,
singing and praying,
fathoming the depths of peace.
And we ...
we rush from stroke to stroke
as the pendulum swings.
In the smoldering mists of time
religion labors and waits
in open searching.
As drafts worry the flame,
the wick sustains the fire.

NEGOTIATIONS

When history turns away from courage
– because of fear –
what is left?
The tit for tat of international politics involves
the most primitive emotions of the species.
And so ...
a few lives
– more or less –
always make a difference:
It
(the difference)
feeds the monsters and the angels.

OUR CITIES

A potpourri of moving things,
forms and sounds, shapes and meaning,
an abundance of life whispering and shouting:
"We are all here now!"
– Immigrants! –
Love them!
For their different colors, smells, sizes,
and their flowered speech.
Love them for their courage!
They may not understand our language or our ways,
nor we theirs.
Be magnanimous!
Those of you who come
and those of you already here.
We are here because we still believe.
They come for the dream.
Encourage them!
We, who are so ignorant of
your ways and languages,
have saved the dream for you.
Learn to live in this confusion of aesthetics!
Buildings of every grandeur,
topiaries of strange creatures,
murals of space and the organic,
and fountains gushing up
sending spirits soaring
are scattered about.
From a primitive moment of imagination,
we emerge.
Out of the darkness you come,
from which I came,
to which we cannot return.
We are all finally on the threshold
of melting into one.

PERMANENCE

I write to add my track of permanence to history.
And yet,
I see the crumbling pages
becoming flakes of brittle sheets
turning to powder
in time's crushing grip.
I wonder,
"What permanence?"
"Where is it?"
I have yet to find a CD
left along the desert trail
consumed by the rays of the sun,
lying shattered,
its integrity, lost in battle with the elements,
giving faint report of any message
contained therein.
And yet,
it is only a matter of time.

SPECIES LOST

By what breach of reason
do we cross faith's threshold
and sink in ageless muck?
As pious animals we turn our minds to pasture
and our backs to fellows of the species.
In the name of righteousness,
sanctimony sets new rules
and we abandon common sense.
As sacred edicts are pronounced,
we clamor in the name
of *Holy Justice*
for the deaths of others.
"Oh ye of craven faiths beware of mine –
'tis holier than thine."
Blinded by our ragings,
stumbling,
we lose sight of reason's shining star.
To right the course
the tiller must be set toward yon brilliant speck.
In all the heavens it's our only hope.
Make straight the way on reason's path
with humble heart and generous spirit.
We know so little.
We pretend so much.

THE BLAME GAME

For the 21st-century person:
the rational, social animal,
the homo faber,
the symbolizing,
freedom-aspiring,
soul-seeking,
sentient being,
the *Blame Game* is a myopic
piece of this century's perspective
that spoils the mosaic of the present
and precludes our ability
to be honest with our now.
If history is to be the template from which
we set sail in the present,
it must be accompanied by an
accommodating openness
that says,
"Yes!"
to at least a critical mass of the present.
This will not be adolescent.
The trail of history is always moving
towards the horizons of
the *Now*.
To judge the present
only from our historical perspectives
is to deny the fertility
of our current circumstance.
The *Now*
is always and forever
more than yesterday.

THE GREAT HORNED OWL

From his daily perch in a tall cedar
(hers was in another tree)
softly would he call to his mate.
(She seldom answered during the day.)
Quietly
they settled into their daily slumber
with gargles and coos.
Periodically his head would rise,
ears up,
and turn towards an odd noise,
then he'd sink back into his snoozing.
In the late afternoon
he would begin to turn his magnificent face
from side to side and blink his formidable eyes
as he began preening his feathers
and scratching his beak.
Finally,
slowly stretching his mighty wings,
those great soft sails that glide him silently
to his prey,
he readied himself for the night.
In this daily ritual of waking,
preening, and stretching,
I was reminded of Nature's efficient patience
as all things unfold.
He then began awakening calls to his mate.
(She finally responded.)
Suddenly,
they would both take flight
on their way to nocturnal repasts.
There was no insistence that bespoke ignorance
of a Grand Design.
They adhered to Nature's Way.

So very far this was
from the human interchange of
pressures and demands.
In all of this
I saw a glorious timeliness.
A pace of purpose and repose
bounded the reality of each and every day.
There were no weekends of interrupted cadence,
only the forever flowing of one purpose:
Honor life through life itself.
Would it be that we could learn to do the same?
Yet we all attempt to win,
pushing and pulling,
engaged in the epic battle,
searching the depths of our caves.
Then,
finding ourselves standing on the pinnacle
of our highest peak,
full of certainty and overrun by anxiety,
begging for others to acknowledge,
and not caring what anyone thinks.
Sure of ourselves,
we huddle in darkness.
Yet we know,
when lost in the freedom of an orgasmic shudder,
the Eternal Hand shaking us
– again –
Knowing Truth
awaits the ensuing quiescence.
And in freedom's musty contentment
yeses are still held
in the whispers of eternity.

THE VET

Deeds done!
Buddies lost – comrades missing!
Some spared the gruesome sacrifice.
Who's in charge of the mission?
There and then:
A multimillion dollar piece of equipment
under their command.
Here:
a lover who couldn't wait ...
no jobs ...
times have changed ...
no mutual respect.
And so
it came to this ...
The headlines read:
"Death in Ditch ..."
"Self-medicated with alcohol ..."
"Marginalized from the mainstream of life...."
To preserve our country's way,
isn't that why we went?

* * * * *

And still they wonder
why I play taps in the evening
at the flag pole
near the edge of the meadow.

TOUCHINGS

I have squeezed myself
from antechamber to foyer in less than a century.
Meanwhile,
I delighted in sharing
the touchings of my being.
For to whom do we owe our presence?
But to it all!

WHAT IS THAT?

What is that?
It is called silence, child.
I've never heard it before.
What do you think of it?
I don't know, it's so strange –
but it sounds like something is there.
What do you think it is?
Listen!
Wow! I don't know what it is,
but there sure is something there.
Listen again!
It is deep and it keeps on going.
Listen some more!
It goes very far, I don't think it stops,
and it seems to call to me.
Listen again!
There is a rhythm, a soft, gentle movement.
What does it say to you?
It seems to say, "Hello! Come with me!"
It is you calling to yourself.
I like that, I really like that.
I think I will go there again –
often.

WHAT TO DO?

So...?
While riding the synaptic bull,
leaping hither and yon,
jabbing a pointed finger
in this eye and that,
we're catching a case of
Blame Them,
anything, anyone.
Choosing in the now to own one's drift
while cursing history's depths of efforts
is a pitiful pastime.
There is the challenge:
to wait for no man or beast.
To seek nothing is abominable.
To this
I prefer the existential quiescence,
embracing in exuberant passion the all of life,
while leaving a trail
next to the barefoot tracks
of St. Francis.

WHAT WILL WIN?

And so ... you ask,
"What will win?"
To you and all others
I say,
"Have you not felt that sigh?
It comes upon exiting
those wooded and marbled floors
of those grand apocalyptic agoras of our day,
where merchant-dice abound amidst
the glitter of light and mirrors and glass,
when finally our feet touch the earth.
When enveloped in the brilliance of the day,
drizzle of the season,
darkness of the night,
our assaulted senses
in a holy expiational exercise
– again –
(those brief reposes given by life's moments)
smother us in fleeting quiescence
sending rippling through our being a symphony
of biology
resonating with ourselves.
What will win?
Life will win!"

WHISPERING WOMEN

Whispering women …
What burdens you have carried
up history's long hill!
Put them down!
Shout,
"Yes!" for joy.
Dance in the rain!
It has come to pass.
You are free!

WHO WILL SAY …?

As I wander in space and time
far from me
and far from mine,
I wonder,
"Who will say Shaba for me?"
For now I am walking toward my grave
and from deep within a barrel chest I hear,
"Adonai! Adonai!"
"Who will say Shaba for me?"
As ashes are passed from hand to earth
a tinkling of bells I hear,
"Adonai! Adonai!"
"Who will say Shaba for me?"
Shufflings of thousands of feet
beat a cadenced chant and I hear,
"Adonai! Adonai!"
"Who will say Shaba for me?"
The angels and their minions
raise their voices and I hear them,
"Adonai! Adonai!"
Such a wonder!
"Who will say Shaba for me?"

ODE TO AN URN

Whose reflection do we see
when peering into the urn's wide mouth?
A glimpse of the shimmering face of the species
flutters on the waters of our time.
The center of ourselves grabs and holds
that vibrant countenance of joy.
Behold! It is us!
In that reality
we call existence,
finding ourselves we exclaim,
"Ah! What wonder!"
"Yes!"
And,
"Thank you!"
A simple visage
penetrates all facades of thought
and cutting quickly to the quick of one,
says, "Yes!"
Then,
in profound silence,
we realize that what is on the surface
offers confirmation of a center.

SHAFTS OF GOLDEN LIGHT

These are:
Late afternoon musings
from the depths of ponderosa shadows.
A trail of life
squandered and exalted.
Through remote canyons,
in hidden valleys,
on slopes of misty mountains,
along banks of gentle streams,
deep within silent swamps,
from edges of alpine meadows,
by shores of Nordic lakes,
standing glistening wet,
come all the machinations of a pounding heart
when moonrises halted briefly
the journey towards
The Truth.

SOUL'S UP!

Soul's up!
Soothed and rattled senses,
slapped and rocked,
caught in a vortex,
laid bare,
shrouded,
bathed in texture,
exploding from edge to edge,
lost and encountering,
my spirit entwined with His
as I knelt in the lee of ponderosas
and prayed.

A LIFE

The myth of politics in the moment
is defined by the whole
as it wobbles on and off course
in some self-serving, self-caring trajectory
of space/time.
The assumption:
a party makes a difference.
The truth is,
it is what's really right that matters
and this is the individual,
either in itself
or in its commitment of another to others.
We all measure time in a lifespan of one.
So …
then it must be that each and every person
is precious,
worthy of every effort
to make of themselves what they can.

WHERE AM I? WHERE IS IT?

We delve into delicious flights of fancy.
Imagination opens its doors and we risk it all.
The savory freedom of others'
purpose and intent
grabs our souls and we succumb
to a search for hidden treasure.
What great needs bend the iron of our hearts
and take us into realms wished for,
hoped for,
sought after?
How is it that a vision so clear emerges
from the turmoil of reality
and settles in tranquil reveries?
And why is it that a gentleness
covers every thing,
hard or soft?
Lost upon a range of fertile vistas
we gladly spend our hours hiding
from God's plan,
or is it when we are so enthralled
we find ourselves strolling in His Garden
in misty mornings and dappled afternoons?
Are these the times when we vaguely see
through the thin film of the present
and gaze upon eternal truths
that light flames birthing dreams?

A REMINDER

A must-made move –
to slum it in the city.

* * *

And then,
a wall,
a rock,
a tree,
a flower,
I take out from my mind's eye
and my soul's pocket
a Zen plate.

* * *

Gosh! It's good!

BROKEN BRANCH

The storm came
and left its calling card,
a broken branch
hung dangling in the wind.
Then it fell –
embracing its beginning.

GIFTS OF LIFE

How do you prepare a mother, a father,
a brother, a sister, for this fact:
It is necessary that their loved one
may have to die
to save the world from itself?
How do we tell them that we must rescue
a people, a gender, caught in a crucible of time
that sequesters souls and squanders lives?
How do we watch the fruits of love,
the flowers of life die
and suffer here,
there,
everywhere?
Is not the measure of our love
the depths of our sacrifice?
The Rauch is up –
a tempest comes.
Prepare the gifts!
Blood will flow.
Life will end.
On the altars
our gifts will be laid
in honor of those who came before
and those who will come after.
Life's mystery boils in the cauldron of time.

GOD'S SOUL

The grand measure of God's Soul
is that in the coalescence of the universe
His heart beats again
and in this thrown-ness into freedom
choice defines our souls.

IT'S A YES! NOW!

Flashing and disappearing,
yeses and nos
come in rapid succession.
The war of yes and no,
always pushing, always pulling.
Sometimes yes winning,
then no having its sway.
Until at last from the din of eternal strife
a hush comes and the softness of an eternal yes
that can be heard from pole to pole,
from planets to stars,
and all across the holy universe.
Life has come!

OTHERS

We watch the movie of the world
from our privileged place of serene ignorance –
choosing to disregard humanity's
pain and suffering.
How is it that we can still feel
"comfortable"
with ourselves and not commit
to an incredible responsibility to others?
This was such an essential hallmark
of our getting here.
Where has it gone?
Has it disappeared into the numbers of our time?
And if this is so,
then why can't we see our neighbors?
What great pile of disregard
or fear
has turned so many into such blind,
uncaring souls?
Does it take a superabundance of courage
just to love a stranger
when they come dressed as we
to the party of life?

LUMBERJACKS IN EARLY SPRING

Apples and oranges are for frogs.
Peelers and axes are for logs.
Ribbons and bonnets are for hogs.
Shotguns and grouse are for dogs.
Half the boys are laughing like a loon.
Half the boys are barking at the moon.
We're all grateful for the tunes.
The cooks, Betsey and Millie, are in the swoons.
It won't be long before we're cooned.
Bags under our eyes are proof we've been babooned.
Mail call hasn't left a Jack without a wound.
The ladies couldn't wait, we've all been gooned.
The numbers are a'growin' with the gout.
Everybody's a'wonderin' what it's all about?
It won't be long before the ice goes out.
Then, if we're still here, we'll all shout:
"Lookey here, boys, spring has sprung!
Just before we climbed on our mind's last rung."
This here is our very late winter song,
and we're still here so nothin's gone wrong.
So that's our song, done and sung.
Just as the Straw Boss says,
"Boys, move that pile of winter's dung!"

MY LAST WONDER

Has my presence helped to cause
another to say, "Yes!"?

A TUNDRIC – PROLOGUE

The word "Tundric" appeared in old Provincial Reports of social import, adding a hint of mystery to the fog of time and the understanding of peoples. As a Royal Canadian Mounted Policeman I could vouch for that. Waxing poetic my mind reflected:

> Much happens in the secret folds of time
> and cliffs of space.
> The depths of life's wonderings
> touch a wide circle,
> and so …
> it's all a circle.

When the inexplicable and profound was described with the phrase "A Tundric," it was always understood to be *more than* what was simply written in the record. Always a silent, reflective respect followed the encountering of the term.

The so-called Deep Ecologists of the day nod soberly, wishing they could fathom the depths and meaning of the interconnectedness of a person's track in time. I know better, and empathize with them.

* * * * *

A TUNDRIC

Peering into black pools
set in a wrinkled countenance,
I asked Falling Feather, an old Inuit,
"Tell me of those Tundric Times."
He nodded and squatting beside the fire,
hands extended,
warming and rubbing his palms,
he began …

* * *

"From under the pelt of the fox and wolf,
nestled in a skin-touching embrace,
senses awaken
connecting us to all the worlds of dreams
and to the cobwebs of our minds.
We wander at the edges of time,
a warm time,
a resting time,
a touching time.
Then,
lost in throes of shared giving,
stretching, reaching, pushing, pulling,
rising up through the roots of the past
to feed the present,
throbbing, pulsating, cascading,
seeds of life
burst into the dark, moist, flowing
caverns of birth."

* * *

He seemed to be in some trance that,
while being here now,
had suddenly placed him
in some remote time and place.

* * *

He continued:
"We greet the day with all of our efforts,
yet the call from behind the now,
through the now,
and ahead of the now,
beckons us to another
Tundric Place.
Ancient firs shiver under stroking hands.
From eons of waiting and wanting,
a fragrance is released
through bent and broken needles.
I am swept up,
lost to time in primordial memories.
Murmurings of silence
from moaning rivulets wanting to be seen
and groaning rivers begging to be crossed
send chilling messages,
licking perspiration and powdered humus
from my limbs.
Falling deeper into hidden recesses
of rest and want,
I wait.
Finally, in waking
I see coils of smoke rise from gray-blackened embers.
The essence calls out
– again –
"Rise and be off!"
Breaking the hallowedness of time it goes on saying,
"Follow me into the vastness,
I will lead you to the seal, caribou and ptarmigan.
Leave the warmth.
Be touched only
by the freezing fingers of the wind."

Suddenly,
I feel cutting crystals cast against my face
and I hear the Tundric Wind Voice saying,
"Heed the calling of your desires,
meet your family's needs,
follow the necessities of life
into the fading gray of the dawn.
Uncover in the forever twilight
the Gifts of Tundric Magic."
I rise and leave her side.
The seal basks but briefly
before the watchful eyes of brother and sister bear.
To feed her cubs she searches relentlessly.
And I
– to feed my own –
must move with the purpose of all life.
In dying the seal gives a coat and flesh
so that we all may live.
Would it be
that they could come in an unending stream
to the door of my shelter!
The chinook salmon must laugh at my thoughts
as they struggle up the crashing waters
to leave their red buttons of life lying scattered in the shoals,
futures forgotten among the pebbles
in the sand.
Life is always a reaching, striving,
a belonging from self to others.
And if I did not take of the other
it could not be as it is for self and my own kind.
All swirls in a Tundric Mosaic as the newest of my kind suckles
warmth and life
from the fountains of my mate.
I touch her and nod,
smiles drip from the corners of her eyes
and linger about my lips.

She knows I must leave.
Gathering the necessities for my journey,
I slip into the white black gray of the arctic day.
Leaving the edge of the forest,
I touch again the needles of the fir.
Taking one,
I crush it beneath my nostrils to catch
the essence of its life.
On my hunt I will smell only myself
in the pasty, arid breath of winter
until my knife slips into the body of my quarry.
Silently,
I make my way farther onto the sheets
of broken ice where they lie
crushed into valleys and mountains,
forever heaving, always different,
forever the same.
Feeding images of flowing white,
severed and cracked, piled up and cast down,
jagged and smooth, brittle and solid,
saying so much in births and deaths.
I reflect upon the rhythm of my passages
always pulling, always dragging,
shoving my family's needs on a sled,
or carrying them into white or verdant wilderness,
south for the salmon, north for the seal,
and always the caribou.
For this is the fabric of our Tundric Sustenance.

* * *

Weeks pass and I have yet to find a seal.
It must be soon, my stores are almost gone.
I think of the enjoyment and vigor I felt
upon leaving my family in search of food.
As days stretch into weeks
and my seeking ends in vain,
I take up my amulet and speak again to the seals.

I know that if death comes in my waiting,
I fear it not.
My only thought is:
"Will there be enough food
until the thaw of Spring
brings grouse and rabbits to her snares?"
The blowing snow encrusts my eyes.
I have no energy to move on.
I can only huddle by an old blow hole
and continue my vigil.
The wind dies and tiny ice crystals,
forming as I breathe,
drop like infinitesimal bells
tinkling in the twilight.
The seals will not come until the morrow.
I must wait yet another night.
Stars share their presence.
The moon busies itself creating shadows.
Wrapping my worn sealskin parka about my body
and burying my face behind its wolfskin fringe,
I drift into a world of memories and dreams.
Melting into the snow
I become one with the ice and silence.
Drifting in and out of sleep my mind reaches back
through many seasons,
and I wander in different places.
In the stillness of my time
and the weakness of my heart,
I call forth the deep pain of the Great Loss,
the Carried One,
the Desired One, the Hoped-for One,
the Lost One.
Lonesome hunts,
intimate moments of family sharings
in Spring gatherings
present themselves in a vast array of days.

My mind lingers – joy rising
from visions of smiles and laughter,
breaking bonds of solitude and pain.
Reunions were times when brother and sister
reveled in the knowledge
that another circle of the sun had held us all
and we were well cared for in our great
Tundric Embrace.
The low-pitched growling of the wolf becomes
the high-pitched cry of the eagle.
I awaken from my slumber.
Truth drives daggers into my eyes.
Two seals bask side by side.
In one swift, leaping, plunging motion,
I impale them both on my harpoon.
Heaving in their death struggles,
I am tossed and beaten against the ice.
My only thought is to hang on to protect the kill,
it will be the lifeblood of my family.
Finally,
battered and exhausted,
they lie still in a vast pool of crimson snow.
Panting in fatigue and ecstasy,
I revel in my
Tundric Moment.
Then
a weariness seeps into my bones
and yet I know brother bear can scent a kill
for miles.
I unsheathe my knife and disembowel my kill.
This all could be used
and yet I cannot take the extra weight.
With thankfulness I eat the warm heart of the large male.
This is a time of satiation and peace,
yet there is no rest.
I must move my treasures from this scented site.

With great effort I roll them onto my sled.
Then lashing them securely,
I begin my long journey back to my family.
Drifting in and out of my senses,
I pull my precious cargo through
the great white sea
while feasting upon my memories.
The hoped for and the called for
gathered around the fires
and peered into the face of the moon.
They had come and many tears of joy fell,
moistening the swaddling surrounding
new gifts of children.
The cold dampness of the days
warmed by the heat of life
slowly evaporate into the autumn's fading light.
"Life is alone together,"
the old men said.
"The bridge to one's self
is over water and over land,
always one to the other."

* * *

Falling Feather seemed to return from his dream
and yet he went on.

* * *

"True life only happens in sharing
with others of our kind.
Everything else happens along the way."

* * *

Profound quotes from some existential philosopher
had never said it better.
I smiled at the old Inuit
as he looked into the gentle licking flames
of the small fire.

Then,
he was lost again in a remembrance
of some other Tundric Time.
Where were the simplicities of these
Other Times
in the world of our day?
How could we capture this sense of sharing
as we scurried through our lives
always besought by an omnipresent rush
of too many things to do
and too little time to do them?
Schools and degrees, children and jobs,
an endless stream of growth,
hers, theirs, and mine,
as well as commitments to others.
This balance of personal aspirations,
family needs,
necessities of social intercourse,
and economic viability seems to be so elusive.
There was always the next season,
next appointment,
always a disappointed cacophony
of competing obligations.
Then,
I recalled the howl of the wolf
and the roar of the bear.
Perhaps our perceptions of those
Simple Times
were never as tranquil as the distance of imagination
leads us to believe,
or we want to believe.

* * *

A vibrating cell pulls me from my contemplation
and I answer my phone:
– An urgent call from dispatch –
"Return to base!"
I turn to give my goodbye to Falling Feather
and realize
he is beyond the current moment
lost somewhere in a Tundric Embrace
remembering a journey of yesteryear,
some forgotten episode
from the patchwork quilt of his life.
I bow to his presence and turn away
to return to base.
Arriving,
I pass through the entryway and hall.
The buzz is about a downed plane.
Rumors are confirmed when
again
the captain says,
"We must mount up, and in a hurry!"
I call from the airport
and let my wife know that I will be gone,
that I love her
and the little ones.
"Such a lack of profundity and of rituals
when lives are on the line,"
I murmur as my mind leaps ahead
to the task at hand.
Boarding the provisioned plane,
I whisper half a prayer:
"Thank God for the DeHaviland Otters,
any place, any time, they labor at their tasks."
As if a prayer to them would save us.
They were the working-man eagles of the skies.
Skimming from lake to lake,
"puddle jumping" the old-timers called it.

They served us well.
The mission was outlined in general strokes,
to be filled in
as we approached our destination.
An unmarked and unscheduled
aircraft had entered Canadian Air Space
and then disappeared.
Our task,
find it and find those aboard.
This was not so unusual in the times
of drug drops,
illegal immigrants,
and the thriving international trade
in animal parts.
We reviewed the coordinates
and marked our maps.
As we listened to the various scenarios
that might play out,
we selected from the plane's stores
the things we knew would be essential
for a wilderness search and rescue,
or apprehension,
as the case might be.
There were three of us.
We would fly a 30-kilometer circle
around the last known coordinates.
Each one of us was dropped at a
one-third circumference point.
Our mission was to converge by a zigzag
route to the spot
where the plane had dropped off the radar.
The Otter would fly a grid over the site
and keep us informed of any sitings.
When the fuel gage said "head to base"
they would so advise us
and inform us of their estimated return to site.

SOP given the size of the plane and its location.
We were each set down at our landing sites
and saying our,
"Meet you at the fire!" goodbyes,
we all started *lining out,*
setting our sights on any anomalies in the terrain.
Always in the back of our minds
a simple truth lingering,
"Who would be the first at the *find?*"
As the magnificence of the vast Canadian wilderness
stretched out before me,
my mind turned to the meeting
with Falling Feather.
We had been brothers for some ten years,
ever since I had stumbled upon him
sitting next to a fire
on the bank of a small stream
in the farthest reaches of the Yukon Territory.
I had stood still and waited
for the old man to return
from his mind's wanderings
before approaching him
to ask how he was.
His reply was, "Humpf!"
as he motioned for me to sit beside the fire.
I patiently sat next to the fire
and waited
as the soft colors of the afternoon
faded into the gentle shades of evening.
When several hours had passed
he spoke, saying,
"When the wilderness was young
you walked upon the banks of this river."

Startled from my thoughts,
I rummaged through my recollections
trying to recall
ever having been on these particular riverbanks.
I never had.
I replied, "Humpf!"
He slowly raised his eyes
from the flickering flames
and said,
"Only someone who waits in silence
to be invited to the fire
and then sits in silence at the fire
has been at the fire before."
Gazing into his dark eyes
I saw the reflections
of dancing flames and said,
"My place has always been at the fire."
He invited me to spend the evening with him
and we talked of the majesty
of the Great Wilderness.
We laughed at each other
as we shared the most beautiful things
we had seen in our wanderings.
Mine was holding a Luna moth as large as a bird.
His was catching a flying squirrel.
He acknowledged that he had indeed seen
the large pale-green moths with the translucent spots
on their wings in late summer.
I relayed that I had spent many evenings
staring into the large eyes
of the soft gliders of the night.
He looked at me in my RCMP uniform
and I looked at him in his soft caribou skins.
He silently held his hand out to me
and I took it.

He said,
"We are both warriors of our kind,
you of yours and me of mine,
yet we speak of gentle happenings
as our favorite wilderness experiences.
We are brothers."
From that time on
we had made it a point to sit and share
around the fire
when we were in close proximity.
They were evenings
both of us looked forward to and relished.
Over the years we became the very best
of wilderness brothers.

* * *

The boulder looked solid on the bank of the river.
I placed my boot on it to position myself
to leap to the next rock
in preparation of stepping
to the log that spanned the rushing water.
Then,
as with most accidents,
I found myself in midair
falling straight down
towards the boulders beneath the log.
The fall was some six meters.
Both feet were jammed between two flat stones.
My weight was instantly
thrown backward with tremendous force.
My backpack weighed in at some 25 kilos.
The cracking of the bones was loud
and simultaneous,
the pain excruciating.

Agonizingly,
slipping my arms from my pack,
I saw it drop into the rushing waters and vanish.
Removing one of the stones,
disentangling and straightening each foot
as well as lifting one leg at a time
took several hours.
I cannot recall how many times I blacked out.
My left leg was broken below the knee.
It was a compound fracture.
My right leg was broken above the knee.
And blessings of blessings
neither had broken through the skin.
I was most fortunate.
From a sitting position,
I inched myself backwards
towards a slender strip of gravel
next to the edge of the water.
Sweating profusely,
two thoughts dominated my mind:
setting both legs, and hypothermia.
I had been sweating as I climbed down the canyon
to cross over the river,
and the ordeal of the moment poured more water
from my system.
The evening would be cold.
Spring comes late in the North Woods.
Behind me and not very far off to the right
were some leaves and twigs
lodged amongst the rocks.
In my sitting position
slowly I backed myself over to them
and leaning over, reached for them.
Gathering all I could,
I piled them around me.

Several of the branches would be suitable
for splints.
My right leg would have to wait
for heavier material.
I built a small fire
knowing that this night
it would have to be tended often
as there was not sufficient kindling
for a large blaze.
Lifting my left leg and placing my foot
between two solid rocks,
I positioned my hands at my sides
and wrenched backwards.
What I heard was an unmanly scream,
or so I told myself as I glanced about.
What difference would it make?
And besides it might bring badly needed help.
On second thought the wilderness responds
to cries of pain.
Glancing about I reflected,
"Why are we so self-conscious?"
The foolish pastimes we feel are so important
mean so little.
I busied myself trimming the ends of the four sticks
I had chosen as splints.
I did not need any abrasions or bruising.
Carefully I lashed each splint to the next,
slowly encircling my leg.
Finally,
there was only a dull fire of pain
where before each movement was greeted
with a sharp stabbing fire.
"To do or not to do,"
I paraphrased the Bard.

The fact was,
the sooner both legs were set,
the sooner the healing could start.
I slowly dragged myself away from the kindling store
towards the top of a tree
that had toppled down the bank of the river
some 20 meters away.
Reassuring myself that I could look forward
to a restful night next to the fire,
I dragged myself along the rock-strewn bank.
Each hunching, dragging motion
sent driving pain into my right leg.
Gritting my teeth against the pain,
I determined to make three lunges
and then rest
breathing deeply for ten long breaths.
This was the formula I used to get there.
One, two, three,
and then with eyes closed and panting,
I counted to ten.
Again and again I repeated this sequence
concentrating only on my next number.
It wasn't twenty meters,
it was only three hunches and ten deep breaths
followed by three hunches
and ten deep breaths.
Survival training had kicked in and
I was focused on the task at hand:
keep on moving.
The goal was to get there.
Time was irrelevant.
In any case my watch had been ripped off
as I slipped my pack off
and it was flung into the river.

I can only guess how long it took
to get to the tree top.
It truly is a wondrous thing
when we can divorce ourselves from conventional time.
"Be present in the present,"
they used to say during our martial arts training.
Once there,
I treated myself to a rest.
Then,
as Edison would do after his mini-naps,
I took out my pocket knife.
"Thank God for the Swiss!
If I could only use the can opener …"
I laughed.
Humor's good for the spirits, or so they say.
I then set about selecting four branches
long enough to serve as a travois for my leg.
I was reasoning that by making the splints
a length that would support
the whole leg,
I could roll and turn as I navigated my way
across the terrain.
Repeating the process used to set my left leg,
(with a manly moaning roar – such hubris!)
I then created the splint for my right leg,
except instead of lashing the splints
only four times
I lashed them six times,
hoping that would be enough to keep the bone from moving.
And then I thought, "Enough for what?"
I knew I could not go west
into the high mountains
although that would be the shortest route
to civilization.

I had to follow the lay of the land southeast
where according to my recollection
and the map that was now somewhere
downriver with my pack,
there was a road some 50 or 60 kilometers away
running northeast to southwest.
That was the goal and if I could make
a kilometer or two a day
it would take about 5 to 6 weeks
to get there.
I hunched myself backwards to the kindling store,
and taking my matches from my vest pocket –
I had always made a habit of carrying
a small container of matches there –
I relit the fire.
I remember Falling Feather saying,
"With knife and fire
a man could weather any storm."
Suddenly
I was overcome with anger.
Why me? Why both legs?
Would I be able to make it out?
Could I survive on what I could find?
Would the Force find me?
Then I started with a litany of *ifs:*
if I hadn't fallen,
if I had only broken one leg,
if the Force found me tomorrow.
Falling Feather's words echoed in my mind,
"Anger with *ifs* has no meaning."
The profound facts of the matter are obvious:
I am here now.
Zigging and zagging
towards the coordinates would
have taken me three to four days.

The team would have waited a day
or two for me at the site.
And certainly with no radio contact
some preparations for rescue
would have been under way.
Members of the team
would have started tracking from
my point of beginning.
Did I leave enough sign?
There were times when my mind had wandered
and I could not be sure my blazes
would have been sufficient.
Besides,
even if they found one it would take time,
circling to cut a zigzag trail.
To follow my trail would be difficult,
if not impossible.
The team would certainly not give up
and they would engage indigenous trackers
to assist them.
Even so,
they could not know
if I was injured or dead.
My mind began to fade.
I put some more wood on the fire and fell asleep.
Periodically during the night,
I stirred and placed more wood on the coals.
Light came late to the canyon
and when I finally awakened
I was accompanied by a dull throbbing pain
that seemed to cover my entire lower body.
I didn't need food immediately,
but it was not something I could ignore.

The fact that fish in the river
were my best
and most accessible source of food was
of paramount importance.
Along with my match container
I had a small length of fishing line
and several hooks
I always carried in my shirt pocket.
After stoking the coals
with several pieces of wood,
I was determined to try to roll over
and crawl back to the water's edge.
My good leg and knee
provided sufficient leverage
for me to turn over.
By putting my hands on the ground
and with a three-point stance
angled to my left,
I could get enough purchase to actually drag my right leg
along on the travois.
To my surprise only if there was a sudden jar
did I feel any sharp pain.
By holding my lower left leg up,
and using my knee
with my two arms,
I was able to haul myself
down to the water in no time.
I thought,
"This is doable!"
Rolling back into a sitting position
I began turning over the adjacent rocks.
In less than a minute I managed to find a grub.

Placing the hook through its lower body
so as to give it an opportunity to squirm,
I threw my line into the river.
It was delightful when almost immediately
a trout took the bait.
Hand over hand, I brought in a nice trout,
about 15 centimeters,
and had him flipping and flopping
on the rocks next to me.
I determined to try again
before I crawled back to the fire.
I took the trout off the hook
and checked to see if the grub
was still in good shape.
It would do.
I threw it in again allowing it to bounce
along the bottom
for some 3 meters when another trout hit.
"Yes!" I shouted,
"This is the way it is supposed to be,
one cast, one catch."
Fishing was not my passion, hunting was.
From the time I was seven or eight
I was hunting squirrels and rabbits.
What I would give for my break-down .22
or even my service revolver that were now
someplace along the riverbank in my pack,
or it had bobbed its way down the river for miles.
I doubted I would ever see them again.
In any case
as soon as I broke out of the canyon,
I would leave the river and head straight across the muskeg
working my way down to the road.

I recalled when I studied my map
the river exited the canyon and began
a series of looping horseshoes and I thought
the best route lay straight southeast.
Here and there I would encounter snowdrifts
that had endured the encroaching spring.
They would be a source of water
as I made my way out of the wilderness.
Periodically by touching base
with the river for food,
I hoped all would go well.
This all sounded like such a good plan
as I sat by the fire
enjoying my delicious meal.
I had laid a flat stone
in the center of the bed of coals,
heaping coals around the stone,
and broiled the catch.
I spent the rest of the day drying my clothes
and arranging my small assortment of provisions.
Not much,
a knife, matches, a fishing line, hooks
and three cooked trout that I stashed
in the back pouch of my jacket.
The following morning
I slowly started down along the riverbank
using my same three point stance
holding my lower left leg up and dragging my right leg.
I remembered the words of Falling Feather,
"Life is always a choice."
My choice was to make it to the road and home.
I followed the river for five days,
stopping in the evenings to fish and build a fire
to warm my spirits as well as my fatigued body.

Leaving the mouth of the canyon
early on my sixth day,
I scaled the remnants
of a dying drift struggling against
the onslaught of an early thaw.
From this vantage point I could better see across the open and
broken patches of muskeg.
A small vale was visible trailing off
towards the rising sun.
There,
as if centering my vision,
was a small rivulet coursing its way to the sea.
Nothing stood out in my panoramic view,
nothing distinguished itself as different
in the endless expanse.
But wait!
Near the edge of the water at some distance
was a small pile of stones.
"A cairn!"
my voice blurted,
as my mind sought to refine the small detail
on the vast landscape.
My heart pounded anxiously in my chest.
A sign that others had passed this way!
I let my body slide down the slippery,
sun-soaked side of the drift
and continued to slowly drag myself along,
conserving my strength as best I could.
It took some time to reach the cairn.
Finally,
there it was right before me,
a mark left upon the land by some long-ago
brother or sister
telling of their passing and giving notice to others
that this had been their path.
Could this also be mine?

Lying with my face resting
on the small stone pile,
my breath coming in shallow gasps
with eyes closed to the morning sun,
I sought to touch the presence of this helpful soul.
"Within! It is within!"
The voices of the ancients spoke to me.
Opening my eyes and turning my head slightly,
I peered into the pile of stones.
"There is nothing but more stones,"
I answered respectfully.
"It is within,"
the voices repeated.
Carefully I started to disassemble the cairn
and lay the stones about on the ground
placing them so they could be returned
to their rightful places.
Having removed ten stones
I was left with five in a circle
with one flat round stone in the center.
Slowly
I raised the center stone
and there below was a small sealskin pouch
nestled in the gravel.
Reverently
I lifted the bag out
cradling it in my gloves,
then, removing my gloves
and carefully untying the thong
holding the bag closed,
I gently tipped the contents into my hand.
A walrus tusk slowly slipped
out of the slender bag.
Setting the bag down
I turned the tusk and as my fingers
ran down the inside curve they discovered carvings.

Recognizing the ancient symbols
of Falling Feather's people,
I could understand them!
Step One was "Play one!"
What was this simple message,
some piece of a child's puzzle, a game?
My eyes owned again the symbols
checking to see if they had registered correctly.
One "Play One!"
There was no doubt in my mind
that is what they said.
I peered off into the paling morning sky
trying to see with my mind's eye
the significance of such a message.
No sense emerged from the symbols on the tusk.
Replacing the carved relic to its home
in the pouch
and laying it beneath its cover stone,
I put the stones back into their proper places
in the cairn.
I lifted my gaze towards the horizon
and asked myself,
"How far was I to drag myself
before I encountered another of my kind?
In which general direction should I go?"
My mind chided me,
east by southeast was still
the best opportunity to find my way home.
For days I continued to pull myself along,
skirting the rugged ground as I moved slowly,
stopping to rest when needed
and spending the nights huddled next
to a tiny blaze.
Fish stood me in good stead.

* * *

And so it was that I crossed over into the
Tundric Moment of my time.
Cutting with the river as it wound its way south,
I crawled my way southeast.
Water was abundant
and for that I was most thankful.
I continued to follow the soft disappearing snow.
My arms and shoulders were not aching now.
When I had started dragging my body along
they hurt beyond any previous effort
I had ever made.
I knew that if I stayed in one spot
the chances that wolves or a bear
would find me would be high.
I also knew I must get off the muskeg and into the forest
where some form of protection
would be available.
As I crawled and rested
and crawled and rested again,
my mind returned to the cairn
and my eyes kept sweeping the edges of the vale.
Suddenly,
there as the sun was closing the curtain
on my thirteenth day,
caught in the depths of a premonition,
I saw another trail cairn
on the other side of the small stream.
Why had they crossed the stream?
What reason would there be
for wading through the cold water
and in my case crawling across
and drenching my entire body?
I had been pondering the cryptic message
discovered at the first cairn
and I wondered if there might be another
buried beneath this one.

I inched my way down to the water's edge
and upon reaching the clear flowing water
realized I had not had a drink for an entire day,
and if I did not drink
I could not maintain my strength.
I drank deeply of the cool, clear water
and slowly felt strength return to my body.
I looked around to find the best place to cross
the mere sled-length of water,
and right there I could see just below the surface
someone had placed flat stones
where one could step lightly
and not be bothered by the water.
I thanked my brother or sister for their thoughtfulness
and yet did not think that it would help me
in my current circumstance.
I hunched myself up on my good knee
and dragged my other leg.
By placing my hands on the stones I reasoned
I could cross without getting my entire body soaked.
Following my three-point stance
and sliding from one rock to another,
I made it across
to the other side of the rivulet.
I then made my way up to the marker.
Again I heard voices saying,
"It is within!"
Repeating my reverent procedure
adopted at the first cairn,
I slowly disassembled the marker to the last circle of stone and
there found another flat center stone.
I gently removed it and to my delight
saw another seal-skin pouch.

Untying the thong and emptying the contents,
another walrus tusk,
into my hand,
I quickly turned it around
and found more symbols.
They read:
Two "Stand Still in Silence!"
"Two," then I had not missed any markers.
I read the symbols again
searching for any meaning.
Then,
repeating the first, "Play One!"
and then the second
"Stand Still in Silence!"
I tried to fathom some deep meaning
and yet there seemed to be no connection
between the first childish admonition
and the second
which seemed to be some kind of warning.
I looked about,
saw the seemingly endless expanse ahead of me.
I could think of no threat
except the possibility of an animal attack
upon the people who had left these messages
so carefully hidden inside the cairns.
Retracing the steps of my previous ritual,
I replaced the tusk in its pouch
and replaced the stones
exactly as I had found them.
As the days passed
I continued to drag and crawl my way
along the small stream.
My mind began to churn over and over
on the messages
trying to glean their precise meaning.
None was forthcoming.

Evenings were spent counting the days
and reminiscing the tracks of my life
and my most recent days.
I had, upon the fourth day,
found a small piece of polished driftwood
along the river and had kept track of the days
by cutting a small notch for each one.
From the small pack I carried on my back,
I removed a tiny portion of my remaining food.
I had been traveling only for two days before
I had fallen between the rocks
and broken my legs.
An embarrassing thing for a Mountie
trained in survival
and especially since I was on a
search and rescue mission.
Finally,
having put my meaningless pride aside,
my challenge had become to survive.

* * *

I continued on for 25 more days,
finding cairns as I went.
Now I had been traveling for some five weeks
and there had been seven in all
with a peculiar message hidden inside each one.
The third had read:
"True / Not True – Mine / Not Mine"
This was as ambiguous as the first two.
The fourth was no less so:
"Own It Now"
It seemed almost comical.
What was there for me to "own,"
crawling and dragging myself through the wilderness
in an all-out attempt to save myself?
The fifth seemed to have
a more profound sentiment.

It read
"Act with Care"
I had read it as "Act in love."
I reread it through streams of tears
wondering how my wife and children
were faring in my absence.
And I wondered what they would do,
especially if I did not make it out?
This love thing was as perplexing now
as it had ever been,
and yet I knew at some deep level that here,
someplace along the trail,
were all the answers to life's deepest questions.
I thought if I could just feel it all,
touch it all,
I would be able to gain a deeper understanding
of myself and of life itself.
Or at least enough to know there were answers
if I could just stay focused long enough
to realize what they were.
I rested and reflected that in the weeks
of my journey
indeed all had gone well.
My legs had set – I felt no pain now –
although I knew that I must be careful,
leave my splints in place
until I could put pressure on my legs.
With the aid of a crutch
I had fashioned from a sapling
found along the river,
I was able to stand and take small, quick steps.
Placing my right leg on the ends of my travois splints
and using my crutch as a third leg,
I could put some weight on my left leg
and make a quick step
while moving my crutch quickly to catch my moving weight.

It felt good to be upright
and to see more of my surrounds.
I had been identifying with ground creatures
and snakes.
Its funny how we feel human no matter what our confines.
To be incapacitated the way I was
had led to a deeper appreciation
of our ability to survive –
any other animal with two broken legs
would have been condemned
to death.
I now knew that I would make it out
and barring any horrible catastrophe
would heal well enough to stay in the Force
and run and play
with my wife and children.
And so it was that I found the sixth cairn.
The message was a mixture
of the profound and comic,
at least in my present circumstances.
"Dedicate Yourself to Growth"
What does an adult do with something like that?
We get old, or older,
not always a delightful prospect.
There wasn't any alternative.
Well, maybe to "age with grace,"
as all the literature of the ages had admonished.
Yet no matter how graceful it was,
it wouldn't stop the aging.
Jumping higher or running faster always
become things of the past.
And that graceful thing,
as I hobbled along with my improvised crutch,
seemed to be beyond my reach.
The seventh cairn's message slapped
me right in the face.

**"Follow All the Other Steps –
a Holy Endeavor Is About to Begin"**
At first I wondered what was so holy
about struggling along with two broken legs,
surviving any way I could
as I continued to work my way out
of the wilderness.
Weeks continued to stretch out
and as I had diverted myself from my original course,
knowing full well that the rough terrain
would not permit me to go west,
I had taken a route that would put me far off
any grid the Force would fly.
The cold, silent aloneness had disappeared
and now was all gone.
The present and the sharing of my being
with my complete
"Icon" was all there was.
The steps had become my undecipherable icon,
my path.
I repeated them over and over
with the reverence of an oriental monk deeply lost in a mantra:
"Play One First"
"Stand Still in Silence"
"True / Not True – Mine / Not Mine"
"Own it Now"
"Act in Love"
"Dedicate Myself to Growth"
**"Follow All the Other Steps –
a Holy Endeavor Is About to Begin"**
I saw them all now as an awakening
into a greater truth,
a maturing awareness that indeed
"It"
was all one;
a difficult perspective to maintain as an officer of the law.

And yet
I knew full well when I came home
to the peals of delight
and the radiance of my wife and children,
"the news of the day"
wasn't the only news of my day.
I had come to realize that local news (really local)
concerning myself, my wife, my children,
my work,
my friends, my community
was where my efforts would be dedicated.
My "Holy Endeavor" was truly life itself,
beginning with my own.
I could hear Falling Feather's voice
coming out of the past,
"Go now and do your duty well.
I will wait here for you next to the fire.
Know that I am always with you."
A shiver shot up my spine and a thought
suddenly hit me.
Did he leave these steps for me,
had he gone on ahead to lead me home?
He didn't come looking for me because
he knew where I would be.
He would check the map at headquarters
and fathom that if I was well
I would have arrived at the point of the find.
If I did not I was either dead or injured.
If I was dead
he would pray for the Great Tundra
to wrap me in its arms
and tell me that he would soon join me
and we would travel together with
the Tundric Winds.
He would not be concerned whether
I found the cairns or not.

A work well done
was always a work well done.
It would be there for "others."
He had always said,
"There will always be 'others.'"
And yet I felt that he would know I was not dead.
He would reason
that if I had to travel injured
I would take the path of least resistance.
He was always ahead of me,
already there leading me as always,
leading me to myself and to my family.
The steps were all telling me
there was only one path.
It was always the one I was on,
always leading me to the path to the self.
I was at once
where I was and where I wanted to be,
actually and *potentially*.
It was as the ancient philosophers had said:
The truth was always already one.
The painful and exhausting journey
of harboring strength,
always moving towards the road,
scrounging food,
the entire exercise paled into insignificance compared
to the joyful experience of finding the cairns
and discovering their meaning.
I now knew them all and they were all mine.
In retrospect it seemed so clear.
Every step leading me closer to the only truth
that matters,
whether enjoyed by me
or given by me as a gift to someone else,
all providing eternal joy.
This was all that mattered.

I will join Falling Feather at the fire
and thank him.
The present and the sharing of my being
with my complete circumstance
is all there is.

* * *

The Force had rescued the pilot
and a family of Afghans seeking political asylum
from warlords of the drug trade.
They had posed as mules
and had flown in with 200 kilos of heroin,
all turned over with names, destinations, contacts,
and trafficking routes taken by other mules.
It was, in all, a major break
for the drug enforcement objectives.
The Afghans had done their duty to themselves
and we had done our duty to Canada
and the international community.
I had fulfilled my mandate to myself,
and Falling Feather
had fulfilled his promise to a friend.
As I had discovered
each one of the steps in the cairns,
I had memorized them and repeated them
over and over as I made my way back to civilization.
I had begun each new day as the dawn broke
by facing the rising sun,
reciting each find:
"Play One First!"
"Stand Still in Silence!"
"True! / Not True!" – "Mine! / Not Mine!"
"Own it Now!"
"Act in Love!"
"Dedicate Myself to Growth!"
"Follow All the Other Steps –
a Holy Endeavor Is About to Begin!"

At first I did the ritual
thinking only of my next step
on my journey to heal my legs
and get back to my family.
Then,
as with all true conversions,
as I repeated them day after day,
I began to realize that the seven steps
were not isolated tidbits of ancient lore.
They were far more
than a cultural anthropologist's dream
of finding ancient artifacts.
I wish I could tell you
there was some formulaic, magic moment
that came to me after reciting them
for seven days at the seventh hour,
or some such coincidence
that would serve others on their journey.
It was more wonderful than that.
While watching a small waterfall
in the early morning light
a small rainbow cast a lustrous haze,
and as I witnessed its gentle presence
I was swept up in rapture that at once
pulled me into its midst and enveloped my entire world.
I sensed a peace such as I have never felt
and a realization that everything was here for me
and that I was a part of everything.
The steps coalesced in the mist
into a luminous, seven-point star
and I immediately knew
that each and every one of them
was meant for me personally
at that very moment,
every preceding moment,
and all my succeeding moments.

There was perfection in their simplicity.
I am **One**. I am my **First**.
To
Stand Still in Silence
is to hear everything,
enabling an understanding.
To separate oneself into self
as **True – Mine – Now**
is to be truly alive.
Self-ownership confers the whole truth **Now**.
Love
is when yes is always present.
Growth
towards the center always bespeaks a *more than*.
Being present as a present is
Holy.

* * *

The fanfare of my return subsided
and when I returned to my home
I shared the journey with my wife and my children
and told them I must see
Falling Feather.
They understood.
I found him seated by the fire
next to his kayak in front of his cabin.
I approached and sat by the fire.
Finally,
he asked me how I was.
I said I was fine and asked him
if he had led me home.
He said, "Humph!"
And raising his ancient head
from his fire-gazing pose,
he winked.

* * *

Some time later,
when reveling in the strength and beauty of the Steps,
I thought,
"This is such rich stuff
I'm going to share the Steps
with that young professor
who taught at the academy.
Perhaps he could ..."

* * *

When did we mine such sacred treasures?
What great deeds in space and time
do we commit our souls to?
When ephemeral pathway seconds consume us all?
Where do we find the road map for ourselves?
What words construct the vision of our passions?
How is it that we discover those Sacred Stepping Stones
on paths to gracious hearts?
Why is it that we wonder if we can,
and then we heroically attempt to do?
Who chooses to allow the wind and rain to block our way?
To stay the course
with belief held high
is the greatest deed of all.

www.ingramcontent.com/pod-product-compliance
Lightning Source LLC
Chambersburg PA
CBHW051807040426
42446CB00007B/553